Tom BRADY

By Jim Gigliotti

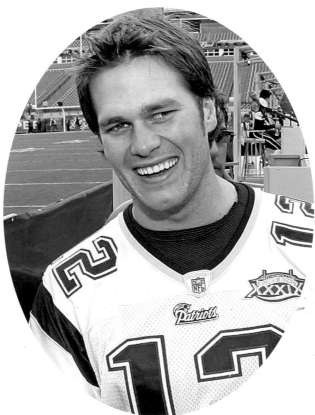

The
**Child's
World**®
www.childsworld.com

Published in the United States of America by The Child's World®
P.O. Box 326 • Chanhassen, MN 55317-0326
800-599-READ • www.childsworld.com

ACKNOWLEDGMENTS

The Child's World®: Mary Berendes, Publishing Director

Produced by Shoreline Publishing Group LLC
President / Editorial Director: James Buckley, Jr.
Designer: Tom Carling, carlingdesign.com
Assistant Editors: Jim Gigliotti, Ellen Labrecque

Photo Credits
Cover: Joe Robbins.
Interior: AP/Wide World: 4; Corbis: 16, 23, 25, Getty Images: 1, 7, 8, 10, 13, 15, 18, 20, 22, 26, 27, 28; Joe Robbins: 3, 14, 26.

LIBRARY OF CONGRESS
CATALOGING-IN-PUBLICATION DATA

Gigliotti, Jim.
  Tom Brady / by Jim Gigliotti.
      p. cm. — (The world's greatest athletes)
  Includes bibliographical references and index.
  ISBN-13: 978-1-59296-794-0 (library bound : alk. paper)
  ISBN-10: 1-59296-794-9 (library bound : alk. paper)
 1. Brady, Tom, 1977——Juvenile literature. 2. Football players—United States—Biography—Juvenile literature. I. Title.
  GV939.B685G54 2007
  796.332092—dc22
  [B]
                                        2006029252

CONTENTS

INTRODUCTION
He Has Nerves of Steel—Usually! 4

CHAPTER 1
Can No. 199 Become No. 1? 6

CHAPTER 2
Drew Goes Down, Tom Takes Over 12

CHAPTER 3
He's a Super Bowl Hero! 18

CHAPTER 4
He's Just One of the Guys, Too 24

CAREER STATISTICS 29
GLOSSARY 30
FIND OUT MORE 31
INDEX AND ABOUT THE AUTHOR 32

He Has Nerves of Steel—Usually!

Pope John Paul II unintentionally managed to do what opposing defenses haven't been able to—rattle Tom Brady!

FINALLY, SOMETHING MADE TOM BRADY SWEAT. Something made butterflies churn in his stomach and made his hands shake.

It was the summer of 2004, and the Patriots' quarterback—the most valuable player of New England's two Super Bowl victories—was in Vatican City in Italy for an audience with Pope John Paul II. "It was the most nervous I've ever been meeting anyone in my life," says Tom, who grew up Catholic.

So there it is. Contrary to popular belief, Tom is not entirely **unflappable**. On the football field, though, he's about the coolest quarterback since legendary Joe Montana of the 49ers.

Montana led the 49ers to four Super Bowl championships in the 1980s. Brady has taken the Patriots to a total of three NFL titles . . . and counting.

Like Montana, Brady was not highly thought of coming out of college. And like Montana, Brady is at his best in the most important games and when games are on the line late in the fourth quarter. Montana, of course, is in the Pro Football Hall of Fame. If Tom keeps going the way he is, he'll be there one day, too. And then they'll be comparing future NFL stars to him.

CHAPTER 1

Can No. 199 Become No. 1?

ON A WEEKEND IN APRIL, 2000, TOM BRADY settled in front of his television to watch the NFL draft. That's when the nation's best college players find out which pro team they'll be playing for.

The first day, when the league conducts only the first two rounds of the seven-round draft, Tom's name wasn't called. No big surprise there. Even though Tom had quarterbacked the University of Michigan to a 10-3 record as a senior—including a come-from-behind, 35-34 victory over Alabama in the Orange Bowl that **foreshadowed** future rallies—he was not highly regarded coming out of college. "Poor build…skinny and narrow," one scouting report read. "Lacks mobility and arm strength on the long ball."

Those criticisms had followed Tom since the

At Michigan, Brady didn't have the strongest arm, but he was a good runner and had terrific leadership qualities.

day he arrived in Ann Arbor, Michigan, after a stellar career at Serra High School in San Mateo, California, just south of San Francisco. He split time with other quarterbacks at Michigan, even beginning his final year alternating with young **phenom** Drew Henson (who eventually went on to play with the Dallas Cowboys) before winning the starting job.

"Looking back, that was the turning point of my football career," Tom has said. "I think competing on the practice field was almost tougher than it was on the game field because you always put so much pressure on yourself."

On the second day of the draft, Tom's favorite NFL team, the San Francisco 49ers, drafted

Tom led his Wolverines teammates to a memorable victory in the Orange Bowl at the end of his senior season.

Growing Up Brady

Tom was the only boy in a family of four children raised by Tom and Galynn Brady—but he certainly wasn't the only athlete. In fact, each of his three older sisters also made their mark on the athletic field.

Maureen, the eldest, was an All-American softball pitcher at Fresno State in the 1990s who compiled a career earned-run average of 0.98. Julie was an all-league soccer player in college at St. Mary's, and Nancy played softball at California.

quarterback Giovanni Carmazzi of Hofstra University. "I was so mad," Tom later admitted. Not only were the 49ers his favorite NFL team, playing not far from his hometown, but they also had a history of producing all-star quarterbacks. (Carmazzi would not become one of them, it would turn out.)

Then the Baltimore Ravens selected Louisville quarterback Chris Redman 10 picks later, and Tom fidgeted a little more while sitting in his living room. Other quarterbacks went in the fifth round and early in the sixth round. Would anyone pick Tom?

Finally, the Patriots called Tom's name on the 199th overall selection of the draft. Despite having been passed over for so long, Tom was ecstatic. True,

Patriots fans wondered why their team had chosen Tom Brady when they had a fine quarterback already, Drew Bledsoe.

it wasn't the 49ers, and it wasn't as high as he hoped to be chosen, but he was heading to the NFL.

Not everyone in New England was happy, though. Patriots coach Bill Belichick found himself on the defensive when talking to local reporters about the selection. With several quarterbacks already on the club's roster, including veteran star Drew Bledsoe and 1999 draftee Michael Bishop, the last thing they felt the Patriots needed was another signal caller. "Too many quarterbacks is a lot better situation than not enough quarterbacks," Belichick reasoned at the time.

Tom would use his draft slot as motivation to show everyone in the NFL that they were wrong.

"Personally, I think it was a great selection by the Patriots, and I think he'll prove that," his college coach, Lloyd Carr, told the *Boston Herald*.

Tom soon did just that.

Young Tom Brady

► Was a 49ers' fan who grew up idolizing San Francisco quarterback Joe Montana.

► Sat in the stands at Candlestick Park (he was 4 years old at the time) the day that Montana and receiver Dwight Clark teamed on "The Catch" to send the 49ers to their first Super Bowl in the 1981 season.

► Attended the same high school (Serra High in San Mateo, California) that also produced Pittsburgh Steelers Hall of Fame wide receiver Lynn Swann and San Francisco Giants baseball superstar Barry Bonds.

► Was a highly regarded catcher in baseball who was drafted by the National League's Montreal Expos out of high school.

CHAPTER 2

Drew Goes Down, Tom Takes Over

LIKE MOST NFL ROOKIES—AND PARTICULARLY MOST rookie quarterbacks—Tom spent the majority of his first pro season learning from the veteran players. He got into only one game for the Patriots, even though the team wasn't very good that season. New England won only 5 of its 16 games, and Tom passed the ball just three times.

Still, most people didn't even expect Tom to make the team that year. But he impressed Bill Belichick and the other Patriots' coaches with his leadership, **poise**, and maturity. And what he lacked in arm strength, he more than made up for with good decision-making—perhaps the most critical trait for any NFL quarterback.

Early in his second pro season, Tom ascended to

number two on New England's **depth chart** behind only Drew Bledsoe. Since joining the Patriots in 1993, Bledsoe had passed for a club-record 4,555 yards in 1994, and had led them to Super Bowl XXXI (which they lost to the Green Bay Packers).

But then, in the second game of the 2001 season, Bledsoe got hurt when he took a crunching hit from New York Jets linebacker Mo Lewis. The veteran

Like all quarterbacks, Tom wore special red practice jerseys; those warn his teammates not to tackle him too hard.

Tom didn't look, act, or play like a young player. He was steady from the start.

quarterback burst a blood vessel in his chest and would be out of action for nearly two months. That meant Tom suddenly was New England's starting quarterback.

Most NFL experts figured it was going to be another long season for the Patriots, who already were 0–2. But in his first NFL start, Tom guided his team to a 44–13 rout of the Colts. While it may have surprised the experts, it didn't surprise Tom.

"I've always had high expectations for myself," he said after the game. "I set my goals high. I've been prepared for this. It's not as if they pulled me off the street and said, 'You're starting.'"

Two weeks later, Tom **engineered** the first of many fourth-quarter comebacks, which would become a **trademark** of his career. New England trailed San Diego 26–16 midway through the fourth quarter of a game in Foxboro.

But Tom completed 13 of 18 passes for 130 yards the rest of the way, including a game-tying, 3-yard touchdown toss to tight end Jermaine Wiggins in the final minute of the period. The Patriots won it 29–26 with a field goal in overtime.

That was just a hint of what was to come the

Here's Tom in action during his breakout game, a comeback win over the San Diego Chargers in 2001.

rest of the way. Though Bledsoe was healthy by midway through the season, Belichick knew he had a special player blossoming at quarterback, and he decided to stick with Brady. "I think Tom has a real good personality for a quarterback," the coach said during the season. "He is confident, but not cocky. He is **assertive**, but not overbearing."

It was not a popular choice at the time. Bledsoe was a local favorite, and it's generally assumed that

New England coach Bill Belichick (right) knew a good thing when he saw it and let Brady remain his starter.

Comeback Kid

Much like his boyhood idol Joe Montana, Tom has mastered the art of the fourth-quarter comeback. "He's calm, he's poised, he doesn't crack under pressure," former Patriots tight end Jermaine Wiggins once said.

Entering the 2006 season, Tom had engineered 21 such rallies in his career (game-winning drives to break a tie or bring the Patriots from behind in the fourth quarter or overtime). That includes three such drives in Super Bowl games—something no other quarterback in NFL history has done so many times.

Tom's biggest rally in terms of points overcome was against Chicago in the 2002 season. After the Bears built a 27-6 lead in the third quarter, he passed for 3 touchdowns as the Patriots stormed back to win 33-30. The game-winner was a 20-yard strike to David Patten in the back of the end zone with 21 seconds left. "I'll never forget this one," Tom said after the game.

injured starters take back their jobs when they're healthy again. But Belichick wasn't about to bench Tom after he had led the Patriots to five wins in his first seven games as a starter. And the quarterback came through for his coach by helping New England close the season with a six-game winning streak. The last, a 38–6 rout of Carolina in the final game, gave the Patriots the AFC Eastern Division championship.

No. 199 turned out to be the right choice.

Tom needed all the comeback and leadership skills he had to lead the Patriots to a win in Super Bowl XXXVI.

CHAPTER 3

He's a Super Bowl Hero!

QUARTERBACK TOM BRADY HUDDLED WITH HIS Patriots' teammates in the final minute of Super Bowl XXXVI against the St. Louis Rams. The score was tied 17–17, and there were only 29 seconds to play in the fourth quarter. New England was at its 41-yard line, had no time outs left, and was facing second-and-10. "64-Max-All-In," Tom calmly said.

In football terms, "max" means maximum pass protection for Tom by his offensive linemen, and "all in" means the three Patriots receivers run inside pass routes at different depths.

Tom found his first option on the play, star pass catcher Troy Brown, open over the middle at the Rams' 45-yard line. Brown made the catch in stride and gained another nine yards before going out of bounds at the 36. After a short pass play and an intentional **spike** by Tom to stop the clock, Adam Vinatieri kicked a 48-yard field goal as time ran out to give New England a stunning 20–17 upset victory.

If you watched the game on television, you'll remember analyst John Madden, a former NFL coach, thinking aloud that he would run out the clock and play for overtime. But the Patriots had other plans.

"We felt that we should give our players a chance to win instead of playing not to lose," then-Patriots offensive coordinator (and current Notre Dame head coach) Charlie Weis said.

Brady hands off to Antowain Smith during Super Bowl XXXVI.

"Any time you have a tie game and the ball, you have to try to take advantage," Brady said.

So he completed a short pass to running back J.R. Redmond, then another, and another. Then, as the pressure mounted, he made the big pass play to Brown to set up the winning field goal.

Confetti flew through the air as Tom Brady and the Patriots celebrated winning the Super Bowl for the first time.

The Patriots were the Super Bowl champions for the first time in franchise history. Tom's statistics were not eye-catching—he completed 16 of 27 passes for 145 yards, including a touchdown—but he was named the game's most valuable player. He completed 5 of 8 attempts on the final march (2 of the incompletions were spikes to stop the clock) and, Weis said, "He made every right decision."

Tom was the youngest quarterback ever to lead his team to a Super Bowl victory. At just 24 years old, he already was on top of the football world.

After returning to New England, Tom holds the Pete Rozelle Trophy, given to him for being the Super Bowl MVP.

Tom's Big Moment

New England's dramatic win over the Rams in Super Bowl XXXVI never would have happened if not for a 16–13 victory in overtime against the Raiders in the AFC divisional playoffs that year. It was that game that ensured Tom a place in Patriots' lore.

New England's Cinderella season appeared ready to strike midnight when Oakland took a 13–3 lead after three quarters in a game played in a driving snowstorm. But Tom pulled the Patriots within three points by running 6 yards for a touchdown with 7:52 to play. Then he marched his team to Adam Vinatieri's tying field goal in the final minute. Along the way, he survived a controversial sack (pictured) that was at first ruled a fumble. The call was

changed, though, and the Patriots kept the ball.

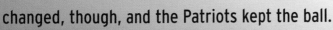

In overtime, Tom completed all 8 of his passes despite driving into the direction of the wind and snow to set up Vinatieri's winning, 23-yard field goal.

A few weeks later, the Patriots celebrated their first Super Bowl win . . . this time indoors!

He's Just One of the Guys, Too

SINCE LEADING THE PATRIOTS TO THEIR FIRST Super Bowl victory in the 2001 season, Tom has become one of the NFL's biggest stars. He earned his second Super Bowl most valuable player award when he guided New England to a 32–29 victory over the Carolina Panthers in game XXXVIII at the end of the 2003 season. The next year, the Patriots won it all again by beating the Philadelphia Eagles 24–21 in Super Bowl XXXIX.

Though Tom has a reputation as the ultimate team player, he's still managed to post some impressive statistics. From 2002 to 2005, he and the Colts' Peyton Manning were the only two quarterbacks to rank among the NFL's top 10 in both passing yards and touchdown passes each season.

In 2005, Tom led the league by passing for a career-best 4,110 yards.

But there's a lot more to Tom's life than just football. Not only did he meet the Pope a few years back, but he was invited by President George Bush to attend the annual State of the Union address in Washington, D.C. He's chatted on television on dozens of TV talk shows, too. He has poked fun at

One of the cool things about being a Super Bowl hero? When you go to Disneyland, they put on a parade for you!

himself on *Saturday Night Live*, done ads for credit cards and watches, and asked if we've "Got Milk?" He was named one of *People* magazine's "Most Beautiful People" for 2002, and posed for *GQ* magazine.

That's only a partial list of the non-sports stuff. They even talk about Tom regularly in the gossip

In His Own Words

After leading the Patriots past the Rams to win Super Bowl XXXVI in the 2001 season, Tom's biggest challenge may have been adjusting to life as a sudden celebrity. He's stayed grounded by focusing on what's really important. He told *The Sporting News*:

▶ *"Football is very important to me, but it is not the only thing in my life. It is something I do. It is not who I am... My life ultimately is about the relationships I have with my family and my friends. As long as those things are in place, all the other things, including football, take care of themselves. But any time you let things get in the way, the distractions—I guess fame is the word—then you start losing your relationships and it starts affecting lots of other things. I can't let that happen."*

columns in Boston newspapers. Of
course, when you date a Hollywood
star such as current girlfriend
Bridget Moynahan and aspire to a
career in politics one day, that's no
surprise. Tom's also a regular on
the golf course, where he plays at
events such as the famous AT&T
Pebble Beach Pro-Am in California
or in a **foursome** with former
Presidents George H.W. Bush and
Bill Clinton.

Sometimes when a player
gets so much exposure, it creates
problems between him and his
teammates. But not Tom, who
would rather be thought of as just

**Actress Bridget Moynahan is often
seen with Tom at movie events.**

one of the guys. "He's not phony, and his teammates
know it," Patriots owner Robert Kraft said.

Tom pulls pranks in the Patriots' locker room—
but more often is the victim of them, too! He passed
up an chance to test the **free-agent market** by opting
to re-sign with the Patriots in 2005 for considerably
less money than he could have made elsewhere.

"My parents raised me in a way that I'm always thankful for what other people are doing," he once said. "One thing you realize when you play a team sport is that everybody, not just one guy, is responsible for any success you may have. I don't think I've ever lost sight of that. Nor do I think I ever will. The reasons we've been successful in New England are because of a lot of sacrifice and a lot of hard work by a lot of people. It's certainly not a one-man band. I feel lucky to be a part of it."

How important is family to Tom? One of the first people he sought out after a Super Bowl win was his father.

Tom Brady's Career Statistics

BORN: August 3, 1977   **BIRTHPLACE:** San Mateo, California

HEIGHT: 6-4   **WEIGHT:** 225

COLLEGE: Michigan   **DRAFTED:** Sixth round, 2000

Year	G-GS	Att.	Comp.	Pct.	Yds	TD	Int	Long	Rating
2000	1-0	3	1	33.3	6	0	0	6	42.4
2001	15-14	413	264	63.9	2843	18	12	91	86.5
2002	16-16	601	373	62.1	3764	28	14	49	85.7
2003	16-16	527	317	60.2	3620	23	12	82	85.9
2004	16-16	474	288	60.8	3692	28	14	50	92.6
2005	16-16	530	334	63.0	4110	26	14	71	92.3
Career	80-78	2548	1577	61.9	18035	123	66	91	88.5

LEGEND: G-GS: games played/games started; Att.: attempts; Comp.: completions; Pct.: completion percentage; Yds: passing yards; TD: touchdown passes; Int: interceptions; Long: longest completed pass; Rating: passer rating, a stat that combines several numbers to create a figure that compares NFL quarterbacks' success.

GLOSSARY

assertive bold, or confident

depth chart in football, a listing of the players showing the starters and backup players at each position

engineered created, built, organized

foreshadowed to indicate something to come

foursome a term in golf for four golfers playing a round together

free-agent market the set of players who can sign with any team during an offseason

phenom a slang term for an especially gifted or promising young player

poise composure, especially in the face of pressure

spike when the quarterback throws the ball down on purpose in order to stop the clock

trademark distinctive characteristic

unflappable calm, not easily rattled

BOOKS

Tom Brady (Awesome Athletes Set 4)
> *By Jill C. Wheeler*
> Edina, Minnesota: Checkerboard Books, 2006.
> Another look at the Patriots' star in a book designed for young readers.

Tom Brady: Heart of the Huddle
> *By Mark Stewart*
> Brookfield, Connecticut: Millbrook Press, 2003.
> A young readers' biography of the Patriots' quarterback.

Tom Brady: Most Valuable Patriot
> *By Stephanie Fuqua (Introduction)*
> Champaign, Illinois: Sports Publishing, 2002.
> Published soon after the Patriots' first Super Bowl championship in the 2001 season, this book is a collection of stories and columns about Tom Brady by the writers of the *Boston Herald*.

Stadium Stories: New England Patriots
> *By Jim Donaldson*
> Old Saybrook, Connecticut: The Globe Pequot Press, 2005.
> A collection of tales about the Patriots and their history, several of which include Tom Brady.

WEB SITES

Visit our home page for lots of links about Tom Brady and the NFL: www.childsworld.com/links

Note to Parents, Teachers, and Librarians: We routinely check our Web links to make sure they're safe, active sites—so encourage your readers to check them out!

INDEX

American Football
    Conference (AFC),
    17, 23

baseball, 11
Belichick, Bill, 10–11, 12,
    16–17
Bishop, Michael, 10
Bledsoe, Drew, 10, 13–
    14, 16–17
Brady, Galynn (mother),
    9
Brady, Julie (sister), 9
Brady, Maureen (sister),
    9
Brady, Nancy (sister), 9
Brady, Tom
    career statistics,
        25, 29
    exposure in the
        media, 25–27
    fourth-quarter
        comebacks, 13, 17
    growing up, 11
    NFL draft, 6, 8–11
    personal views,
        14, 26, 28
    presidents he
        has met, 25, 27
    Super Bowls, 5, 17,
        18–23, 24
Brady, Tom (father),
    9, 28
Brown, Troy, 19–20

Carolina Panthers, 8,
    17, 24
Clark, Dwight, 11

depth chart, 13

free-agent market, 27

golf, 27

Henson, Drew, 7–8

Indianapolis Colts, 14,
    24

jersey, practice, 13

Kraft, Robert, 27

Montana, Joe, 5, 11, 17
Montreal Expos, 11
Most Valuable Player
    (MVP), 5, 22, 24
Moynahan, Bridget, 27

National Football
    League (NFL), 6, 8–11
New England Patriots
    AFC divisional
        playoffs, 17, 23
    Brady with the, 5,
        12–17, 27
    drafting Brady, 9–11
    Super Bowls, 18,
        19–22, 24, 26

Oakland Raiders, 23
Orange Bowl, 6, 8

Patten, David, 17
Pete Rozelle Trophy, 22
Philadelphia Eagles, 24
Pope John Paul II, 5
Pro Football Hall of
    Fame, 5, 11

Redmond, J. R., 20
religious beliefs, 5

St. Louis Rams, 19, 23,
    26
San Diego Chargers,
    14–15
San Francisco 49ers, 5,
    8–9, 11
Serra High School, 7, 11
Smith, Antowain, 20
Super Bowl XXXI, 13
Super Bowl XXXVI,
    18–22, 26
Super Bowl XXXVIII,
    8, 24
Super Bowl XXXIX, 24

University of Michigan
    Wolverines, 6, 7, 8

Vinatieri, Adam, 20, 23

Weis, Charlie, 20, 22
Wiggins, Jermaine, 15,
    17

ABOUT THE AUTHOR

Jim Gigliotti is a writer who lives in southern California with his wife and two children. A former editor with the National Football League's publishing division, he has written more than a dozen books about sports and personalities, including *Stadium Stories: USC Trojans* and *Watching Football* (with former NFL star Daryl Johnston).